Harry Potter Dessert Cookbook

The Magical Wizard Book To Bake Monster Chocolate Cookies, Birthday Cakes And Other Hogwarts Sweets

RACHEL WILLIAMS

Copyright © 2020 by Rachel Williams.

All rights reserved.

No part of this publication or the information in it may be quoted from or reproduced in any form by means such as printing, scanning, photocopying or otherwise without prior written permission of the copyright holder.

This cookbook was made for Harry Potter fans by Harry Potter Fans and is not an official or authorized product. It is not approved or associated with J.K. Rowling and/or her publishers.

Harry Potter, characters, names, films and novel features used within this book are trademarked and owned by J.K. Rowling and Warner Bros Entertainment Inc.

Table of Contents

Hedwig Cake 1

Hagrid Rock Cakes 3

Owl Cupcakes 5

OWL POPS 8

Slughorn's Popcorn Balls 10

Aragog Chocolate Cupcakes 12

Aunt Petunia's Chocolate Cake 14

Hogsmeade Puddings 17

Chocolate Monster Cookies 19

Broomsticks Cup Cakes 21

Hermione's Secret Cake 23

Pumpkin Plumcakes 25

McGonagall's Marshmallow Brownies 27

Molly Weasley's Carrot Cake 29

Hufflepuff's Special Cake 32

Cornelius Fudge Cheesecake 35

Slytherin's Pistachio Cake 38

Hermione's Fudgy Brownies 40

Butterbeer Cake 42

Harry's Breakfast 46

Dumbledore's Pumpkin Cheesecake 49

Quidditch Traditional Cake 52

Durmstrang Famous Cake 54

Ron's Favourite Plumcake 57

Cauldron Cake 59

Durleys's Doughnuts 61

Slug Club Dessert 63

Hogwarts Pudding 65

Pomona Sprout Secret Recipe 67

Gryffindor House Cake 70

HEDWIG CAKE

Difficulty: Easy

Time: 1 hour

Serves: 6 people

Ingredients:

For the crêpes:

- ✓ 500 gr (1 Cup) flour
- ✓ 120 gr (4 oz) sugar
- ✓ 1 liter (4 cups) whole milk
- ✓ 6 eggs
- ✓ salt
- ✓ Orange zest

For the strawberry mixture:

- ✓ 500 gr (2 cups) Ripe strawberries
- ✓ 60 gr (4 tbsp) Icing sugar
- ✓ 30 cl (2 tbsp) Water

Directions:

Let's begin by making the strawberry sauce: wash the strawberries and clean them of any green or unripe white parts.

Cut them into coarse pieces

Put them in a non-stick saucepan, add the sugar and 2 tablespoons of water

Cook over medium heat for 5 minutes making sure that they don't stick to the bottom of the pan.

Put the mixture into the blender and blend well. You can pass the blended strawberries through a sieve to eliminate the small seeds.

For the crêpes, start by mixing the flour with the sugar (The flour must be well sieved).

Add a pinch of salt, the orange zest, the milk and mix with a hand whisk.

In a separate bowl, beat the eggs and then add them to the mixture.

Cook the crêpes in a very hot and lightly buttered crêpe maker or in a non-stick pan.

With these ingredients, you should get more or less 30 crepes (about 20 cm / 8 inches in diameter)

To make all the crêpes in the same size, use a ladle as a measuring spoon, always filling it with the same amount of batter.

Spread a layer of sauce on each crêpe and stack them to form the cake.

Sprinkle the last layer with a generous amount of icing sugar

Hermione's tips:

A crêpe cake can be filled in many ways

Try a classic vanilla or chocolate custard or a tiramisu cream with eggs and mascarpone.

You prefer something lighter? Try using bitter orange jam which is not too cloying and goes very well with the taste of the crepes.

A perfect idea for an after-dinner meal, but also for a snack.

HAGRID ROCK CAKES

Difficulty: Easy

Time: 30 Minutes

Serves: 6 people

Ingredients:

- ✓ 20 gr (4 tsp) butter
- ✓ 100 gr (3 oz) milk chocolate
- ✓ 1 tbsp honey
- ✓ 45 gr (3 tbsp) corn flakes

Directions:

Put the butter and the finely chopped chocolate in a glass bowl and microwave at medium temperature (220 °C/450 °F) for a minute or two.

Add the honey and mix well until a homogeneous mixture is obtained.

Pour the corn flakes in the bowl (and don't worry if they seem a lot compared to chocolate, because they won't be) and mix gently, trying not to crush the cornflakes.

Helping yourself with two teaspoons, shape the mixture into small balls and line them on a baking tray.

Let the cakes thicken in the fridge for about 2 hours before serving.

Hermione's Tips:

To make the rock cakes even tastier, you can add almonds, hazelnuts or dried fruit.
If you prefer the aroma of orange instead, you can add some finely grated orange peel.

OWL CUPCAKES

Difficulty: Medium

Time: 2 hours

Serves: 4 people (8 cupcakes)

Ingredients:

For the base:

- ✓ 45 gr (3 tbsp) flour
- ✓ 20 gr (4 tsp) high quality bitter cocoa powder
- ✓ 60 g (4 tbsp) sugar
- ✓ 45 gr (3 tbsp) soft butter (room temperature)
- ✓ 1 egg
- ✓ 1 teaspoon vanilla extract (or 1/2 vanilla berry seeds or 1/2 sachet of vanillin)
- ✓ 1/2 tablespoon of baking powder

For the chocolate frosting:

- ✓ 150 gr (5 oz) high quality dark chocolate bars
- ✓ 100 gr (3.5 oz) fresh whipping cream

Decorations:

- ✓ Black sugar paste
- ✓ White sugar paste

Directions:

Coarsely chop the chocolate.

Put the cream in a saucepan and bring to boil.

When it starts boiling, turn off the heat, move away from the stove and pour the dark chocolate into the cream.

Turn the mixture with a hand whisk until a homogeneous, smooth, lump-free mixture is obtained.

Leave your ganache at room temperature for about 1-2 hours. Occasionally check the consistency.

Once the Ganache Cream is ready, set it aside at room temperature and dedicate yourself to the Cupcakes

In a container with high sides, add the soft butter, sugar and vanilla.

Use a whisk to whip the butter for at least 5 minutes.

Once you have reached a frothy consistency, add the egg.

Mix the egg and the butter cream at low speed.

In a separate bowl mix flour, cocoa and yeast.

Sift the powders and spoon them into the mixture.

Whisk at low speed to mix the ingredients until you get a creamy, thick and compact mixture:

Arrange 8 cupcake baking cups inside a muffin pan of the same size. Spoon the mixture into the baking cups, filling them a little more than half.

Bake in a preheated oven for 20 minutes at 180 °C (360 °F).

Remove from the oven and immediately take the cupcakes out of the mold and let them cool.

Wait until the cupcakes are completely cold to proceed with the decorations.

Meanwhile, the chocolate ganache should have thickened and should be ready to be used as frosting.

Prepare a piping bag with a star spout. Fill the piping bag with the ganache cream and close well so that there are no air bubbles in the bag.

Start from the center of the cupcake, and circle around the cupcake with the piping bag

To make the eyes, overlap a small dab of black sugar paste over a larger white one

Place the eyes on the muffin covered with chocolate ganache.

For the beak, take a yellow M & M's and place it between the two eyes.

OWL POPS

Difficulty: Easy

Time: 30 minutes

Serves: 6 people

Ingredients:

- ✓ 100 gr (3.5 oz) Oreo biscuits
- ✓ 185 gr (6.5 oz) spreadable cheese;
- ✓ 100 gr (3.5 oz) White chocolate for covering
- ✓ 45 gr (3 tbsp) butter
- ✓ Colored sugar paste
- ✓ Toothpicks straws or plastic sticks

Directions:

Put the Oreos in the mixer and dust them.

Add the cheese and mix.

When you have obtained a homogeneous mixture, roll it into small balls and put them on a plate or on a cutting board and leave to rest in the fridge for a few hours.
If you don't have much time, put the balls in the freezer.

Slowly melt the chocolate and the butter on very low heat (bain-marie)

Remove the chocolate balls from the fridge, stick them with long toothpicks or plastic sticks and dip them in the melted chocolate.

Let the chocolate thicken for a few minutes.

Decorate with the sugar paste and leave to rest in the refrigerator for 10-15 more minutes before serving.

SLUGHORN'S POPCORN BALLS

Difficulty: Easy

Time: 30 Minutes

Serves: 4 people

Ingredients:

- ✓ 60 gr (4 tbsp) of butter
- ✓ 1 kg (4 cups) marshmallows (miniature)
- ✓ 1 bag of popcorn (normal, 12 popped cups)
- ✓ 1 teaspoon vanilla extract
- ✓ 1/4 teaspoon salt
- ✓ 350 gr (1 and ½ cups) of candy corn

Directions:

Prepare a baking sheet by lining it with aluminum foil. Sprinkle the foil with a non-stick cooking spray.

Place the popcorn and candy corn in a large bowl and set them aside.

Put the butter in a microwave for 30-45 seconds to melt it. Add the marshmallows and microwave for another 90 seconds to melt them. The marshmallows may not seem to melt, but once you mix them they should liquefy.

Stir to melt the butter and marshmallows, then add the vanilla and salt and mix until the candies are well mixed.

Pour the marshmallow mixture over the popcorn and candy corns and mix until completely combined. Leave the mixture to rest for a few minutes to cool the hot marshmallow.

Spray your hands with a non-stick cooking spray and collect a handful of popcorn. Press firmly between your hands, forming a ball shape. Make sure the balls are compact; loosely formed popcorn balls come off easily.
If the balls don't form, let the mixture sit for another minute, this seems to help them hold together. Place the popcorn balls on the prepared pan and let them solidify at room temperature.

Store the popcorn balls in an airtight container in a cool, dry room.

ARAGOG CHOCOLATE CUPCAKES

Difficulty: Easy

Time: 2 hours

Serves: 4 people (8 Cupcakes)

Ingredients:

For the base:

- ✓ 200 gr (7 oz) flour
- ✓ 2 eggs
- ✓ 160 gr (5.5 oz) sugar
- ✓ 120 gr (4 oz) butter (softened)
- ✓ 120 ml (4 fl oz) milk
- ✓ 1/2 sachet of baking powder
- ✓ 100 gr (3.5 oz) dark chocolate

To decorate:

- ✓ 120 gr (4 oz) dark chocolate
- ✓ 2 spoons fresh cream
- ✓ 100 gr (3.5 oz) chocolate sprinkles
- ✓ 4 licorice wheels (for the legs)
- ✓ 24 eye shaped candies

Directions:

Start by mixing the sugar and soft butter in a bowl using a hand whisk or an electric mixer to obtain a frothy and whitish cream.

Add the eggs, one at a time, making sure that each is well mixed with the sugar and butter before adding the next.

Melt the dark chocolate over low heat (bain-marie), let it cool down a bit and add it to the mix

Lastly, sift the flour and baking powder and slowly add it to the mixture, together with the milk. Whisk until a smooth and rather thick dough is obtained.

Fill the muffin cups, for 2/3 of their capacity. Then bake the muffins in a preheated oven at 180 °C (360 °F) for 20-25 minutes. When they are ready, take them out of the oven and let them cool completely.

Once the muffins have cooled down, you can proceed with the decoration.

Melt the chopped dark chocolate in a double boiler or microwave, add the hot cream and mix well, to obtain a dense and compact ganache.

Spread the chocolate ganache on the muffins, put the chocolate sprinkles in a bowl and dip the muffin head in the sprinkles, covering it completely.

Finally decorate with strings of licorice wheels (legs) and with eye shaped candies (little eyes).

AUNT PETUNIA'S CHOCOLATE CAKE

Difficulty: Medium

Time: 3 hours

Serves: 6 people

Ingredients:

For the base:

- ✓ 160 g (5.5 oz) flour
- ✓ 75 g (5 tbsp) bitter cocoa powder
- ✓ 8 large eggs at room temperature
- ✓ 240 g (1 Cup) sugar

For the filling and decorations:

- ✓ 750 g (3 cups) mascarpone

- ✓ 750 ml (3 cups) whipping cream
- ✓ 120 g (4 oz) powdered sugar (to be used only if the cream used is not sweetened)
- ✓ 3 generous spoons of nutella
- ✓ 3 tablespoons of bitter cocoa

To wet the cake:

- ✓ Milk to taste
- ✓ Cocoa to taste

For the chocolate ganache:

- ✓ 100 g (3,5 oz) dark chocolate
- ✓ 100 g (3.5 oz) of fresh liquid cream

To decorate and garnish:

- ✓ Candy Corn

Directions:

Let's start by making the sponge cake: It is possible to prepare the sponge cake even a day or two before finishing the cake. Store it wrapped in plastic wrap.

Whip the eggs at room temperature with the sugar and a pinch of salt for about 15 minutes, until a light and frothy mixture is obtained.
Gradually add the sifted flour with the bitter cocoa, stirring patiently with a wooden spoon, always from the bottom upwards.
Pour the resulting mixture, very soft and frothy, into two hinged trays, 22 cm (8.5 inches) in diameter, buttered and floured, or lined with parchment paper both on the bottom and along the entire edge.

Bake in a preheated oven at 180 °C (360 °F), static mode, for about 40 minutes.
Do the toothpick test in the center of the sponge cake to check if completely cooked

Allow the sponge cake to cool completely and prepare the cream for filling: whip the cream together with the icing sugar and then add the mascarpone.

Mix the ingredients well until a thick cream is obtained.

Add the nutella and cocoa and mix all the ingredients well.

After making the basic preparations, start assembling the cake: cut the sponge cake into two layers. Obtaining a total of 4 layers.

Wet the sponge cake, without excess, with milk and cocoa.

Stuff the first layer with the cream, place the second layer on the cream and proceed in the same way with the other layers.

Cover the whole cake with the cream, leveling the cream well both on the surface and along the entire edge.

Place the cake in the refrigerator and prepare the chocolate ganache that will be used to make the drippings. Heat the liquid cream in a saucepan and turn off as soon as it is about to boil. Add the dark chocolate, cut into small pieces.

Stir until the chocolate has completely melted.

Allow the ganache to cool and start pouring. It will be necessary to do some tests to understand the right consistency. If the ganache is too liquid, it will drain too quickly along the edge of the cake and in that case we will have to wait for it to cool a little. Otherwise, if the ganache does not run down the edge it means that it is too cold and you will need to warm it up a little. Start from the edge to make the drippings.

After realizing the dripping effect, cover the entire surface with the remaining ganache.

Garnish the cake with sweets to taste.

HOGSMEADE PUDDINGS

Difficulty: Easy

Time: 1 hour

Serves: 6 people

Ingredients:

- ✓ 170 g (6 oz) sugar
- ✓ 6 large egg yolks
- ✓ 3 tablespoons cornstarch
- ✓ 1 pinch of salt
- ✓ 850 ml (3 and ½ cups) milk
- ✓ 2 teaspoons vanilla extract
- ✓ 100 g (3.5 oz) butter
- ✓ 5 - 8 drops of orange food coloring

- ✓ 350 g (1 and ½ cups) cream (35% fat)
- ✓ 2 teaspoons of icing sugar

Directions:

Put the sugar, egg yolks, corn starch, salt, milk and vanilla in a bowl and mix quickly with a whisk, then cook on low heat for 25 minutes.

Add the butter turn off the heat and mix. Divide half of the pudding into 4-6 cups of parfait.

Cover the cups with cling film directly touching the surface of the pudding and set aside.

Transfer the remaining pudding to a bowl, add the orange food coloring and mix with a spoon until completely blended.

Cover the bowl with cling film by touching the surface of the pudding directly. Refrigerate all puddings until solidified (about 1 hour).

Pour the orange pudding over the regular pudding in parfait cups, creating two distinct layers and set aside.

Whip the cream and sugar until the desired consistency is obtained. Coat each cup of pudding with whipped cream and serve immediately.

CHOCOLATE MONSTER COOKIES

Difficulty: Easy

Time: 2 hours

Serves: 6 people (15 cookies)

Ingredients:

- 240 g (1 Cup) Dark chocolate
- 200 g (7 oz) Milk chocolate
- 120 g (4 oz) Butter
- 150 g (5 oz) flour
- 5 g (1 tsp) Baking powder
- 1 pinch Coarse salt
- 2 Eggs
- 1 Yolks

- ✓ 150 g (5 oz) Sugar
- ✓ 1 Vanilla bean
- ✓ Smarties
- ✓ Candy Eyes

Directions:

Melt the dark chocolate in a water bath or in the microwave and let it cool.

In the meantime, cut the butter into cubes and let it soften at room temperature, then add the sugar and the seeds of the vanilla bean and mix with a blender until a light and creamy mixture is obtained. Add the eggs one at a time while still mixing. Finally add the salt and the melted chocolate, now lukewarm.

At this point add the sifted flour, the baking powder and the milk chocolate, cut into small cubes. Mix all the ingredients and then place the mixture in spoonfuls on a baking tray lined with parchment paper. Cover the cookies with Smarties and Candy Eyes.

Bake in a preheated oven at 180 ° (360 °F) for about 15-20 minutes.

Remove the biscuits with a spatula and place them on a wire rack to cool.

BROOMSTICKS CUP CAKES

Difficulty: Easy

Time: 30 Minutes

Serves: 4 people

Ingredients:

- ✓ 200 gr (7 oz) dark chocolate
- ✓ 75 gr (5 tbsp) whipping cream
- ✓ 10 gr (2 tsp) butter
- ✓ Small aluminum chocolate molds

Directions:

Take each aluminum mold and open it slightly giving the shape of the broom.

Insert a stick carefully and then insert the other end on a piece of cheese or other surface that can hold the sticks upright until the chocolate has solidified.

Melt the chocolate in the microwave or in a bain-marie. Add the whipped cream and butter.

Fill the molds gently with the melted chocolate, keeping them as vertical as possible.

Let the chocolate solidify at room temperature or by carefully putting the molds in the fridge.

Remove the molds and serve.

HERMIONE'S SECRET CAKE

Difficulty: Medium

Time: 1 hour

Serves: 6 people

Ingredients:

For the hazelnut cake:

- ✓ 100 g (3,5 oz) hazelnuts
- ✓ 100 g (3,5 oz) flour
- ✓ 75 g (5 tbsp) butter
- ✓ 45 g (3 tbsp) granulated sugar
- ✓ 1 egg
- ✓ 3 pears

For the hazelnut cream:

- ✓ 75 g (5 tbsp) hazelnuts
- ✓ 45 g (3 tbsp) sugar
- ✓ 45 g (3 tbsp) butter at room temperature
- ✓ 30 g (2 tbsp) 00 flour
- ✓ 1 egg
- ✓ 1 teaspoon of vanilla extract (or half vanilla pod)

Directions:

Prepare the hazelnut pastry by blending the hazelnuts with the sugar (if you want you can use the hazelnut flour and skip this step, mix the flour with the sugar).

Add the flour and the butter into chunks. Mix with your hands until the mixture become sandy and finally add the egg. Continue working the dough until it has the right consistency. Wrap it with plastic wrap and store in the refrigerator for an hour.

Roll out the hazelnut pastry with a rolling pin. Line a tart mold with butter and flour and put the rolled out dough in the mold. Place in the refrigerator.

Prepare the cream by mixing all the needed ingredients in a bowl and add a pear, cut into small cubes. Spread the cream in the pastry shell.

Peel the remaining two pears and slice them. Arrange the slices on the cream. Brush them with melted butter and sprinkle them with sugar.

Bake at 170 °C (340 °F) in a preheated oven for about 30 minutes (until golden brown).

Hermione's Tips:

Do you want to enhance the taste of this cake? Enjoy it with a scoop of vanilla cream ice cream!

PUMPKIN PLUMCAKES

Difficulty: Easy

Time: 90 minutes

Serves: 4 people

Ingredients:

- ✓ 300 g (10,5 oz) Pumpkin
- ✓ 200 g (7 oz) flour
- ✓ 45 g (3 tbsp) Potato starch
- ✓ 3 eggs
- ✓ 150 g (5 oz) sugar
- ✓ 45 g (3 tbsp) Seed oil
- ✓ 250 g (1 Cup) Natural white yogurt
- ✓ 1 sachet Baking powder

- ✓ 45 g (3 tbsp) Chocolate drops
- ✓ Icing sugar (to garnish)

Directions:

Peel the pumpkin, remove the seeds and filaments and boil it or steam it until it becomes soft. Drain the pumpkin and blend it in a mixer.

Whip the eggs with the sugar until they become a clear and frothy mixture.

Add the flour and starch while continuing to whip, then add the yogurt, oil and baking powder. Finally add the pureed pumpkin and mix well until you obtain the correct texture of the dough.

Add the chocolate chips and transfer the mixture into a greased and floured plum cake mold.

Bake your pumpkin plum cake in a static oven, preheated to 175 °C (350 °F) for about 45 minutes, then remove the cake from the oven.

Let it cool for 15-20 minutes, remove the plum cake from the mold and garnish with icing sugar. Serve cut into slices.

Hermione's tips:

If you want a different effect, divide the mixture into two bowls: in one add the bitter cocoa and mix with the whisk to incorporate it into the other ingredients.

Once the plum cake mold has been buttered and floured, pour the two compounds inside, alternating them, in order to obtain the two-tone effect.

MCGONAGALL'S MARSHMALLOW BROWNIES

Difficulty: Easy

Time: 1 hour

Serves: 6-8 people

Ingredients:

- ✓ 150 gr (5 oz) unsalted butter
- ✓ 300 gr (1 and 1/4 cups) sugar
- ✓ 250 gr (1 cup) unsweetened cocoa powder
- ✓ 1/4 teaspoon salt
- ✓ 1/2 teaspoon vanilla extract
- ✓ 2 cold large eggs
- ✓ 120 gr (½ cup) flour
- ✓ 80 gr (⅓ cup) chocolate chips

- ✓ 300 gr (1 and 1/4 cups) small marshmallows
- ✓ 120 gr (1/2 cup) salted almonds, chopped

Directions:

Mix the butter, cocoa, sugar and salt in a saucepot or bowl. Create a double boiler (bain-marie) and stir the butter until it's melted and the mixture is smooth and silky. Remove the bowl from the double-boiler and let it cool for 10 minutes.

Using a spoon or spatula, stir in the vanilla and then stir in the eggs, one at a time, stirring vigorously between each addition. Once the compound looks well-blended, shiny and thick, stir in the flour until it's fully incorporated. Spread the batter into a baking pan, lined with parchment paper.

Bake the brownies for 15 to 20 minutes in an oven, preheated to 160°C (325°F). Do the toothpick test to check if completely cooked.

Remove from the oven and sprinkle with chocolate chips, mini marshmallows and chopped almonds. Return the brownies to the oven for 5 more minutes, until the marshmallows start melting.

Remove the brownies from the oven and let them cool on a rack for at least 15 minutes.

Remove the brownies from the pan, slice and serve.

MOLLY WEASLEY'S CARROT CAKE

Difficulty: Medium

Time: 160 minutes

Serves: 6 people

Ingredients:

For the cake:

- ✓ 350 gr (1 and ½ cup) grated carrots
- ✓ 250 gr (1 cup) flour
- ✓ 20 gr (4 tsp) cashew nuts
- ✓ 20 gr (4 tsp) pine nuts
- ✓ 20 gr (4 tsp) pistachios
- ✓ 20 gr (4 tsp) almonds
- ✓ 4 large eggs

- ✓ 200 gr (7 oz) granulated sugar
- ✓ 100 gr (3,5 oz) cane sugar
- ✓ 250 ml (1 cup) sunflower oil
- ✓ 1 teaspoon of vanilla extract
- ✓ 1 teaspoon ground cinnamon
- ✓ 1/2 teaspoon of salt
- ✓ 1 teaspoon baking soda
- ✓ 5 gr (1 tsp) baking powder

For the frosting:

- ✓ 500 gr (2 cups) fresh creamy vegetable cheese
- ✓ 250 gr (1 cup) icing sugar
- ✓ 180 ml (6 fl oz) liquid vegetable cream
- ✓ 1 teaspoon vanilla extract

Directions:

Start by peeling and washing the carrots; dry them with a cloth and grate them with a small hole grater. Chop the dried fruit with a knife.

In a bowl combine the flour with baking soda, baking powder, cinnamon salt and mix well.

In a large bowl, whisk the eggs (egg white + yolk) with the caster sugar and the cane sugar. Whisk well with an electric whisk or planetary mixer until frothy.
Add the oil to the frothy mixture and work again.
Start adding the powders one tablespoon at a time, incorporating the powders well before adding more.
Finally, add the grated carrots and the dried fruit cut into small pieces.

Oil the mold, or line with parchment paper, and pour the mixture.

Bake in preheated oven, at 180 ° C (360 °F), for 40 - 45 minutes. Before taking the cake out of the oven, do a toothpick test which must come out very dry; otherwise, continue cooking.

Remove from the oven and leave to cool completely before turning out.

Whisk the vegetable cheese to make it creamier. Add the icing sugar and whisk again.

Finally, add the liquid vegetable cream and vanilla.

Work well to obtain a smooth and soft cream, then store in the refrigerator until use.

Once the cake has cooled down completely, gently take it out of the mold and cut it into three discs of equal thickness.

Spread the cream cheese on the first disk, cover with the second disk, and repeat with all three disks.

Decorate with dried fruit, whole or in grains, or with pecans

HUFFLEPUFF'S SPECIAL CAKE

Difficulty: Medium

Time: 150 minutes hours

Serves: 6 people

Ingredients:

For the base:

- ✓ 150 g (5 oz) flour
- ✓ 75 g (5 tbsp) Butter
- ✓ 60 ml (4 tbsp) water (COLD!!)
- ✓ 1 teaspoon apple cider vinegar
- ✓ 1 pinch Fine salt

For the filling:

- ✓ 100 g (3,5 oz) Coconut sugar
- ✓ 45 g (3 tbsp) brown sugar
- ✓ 100 ml (3 fl oz) Maple syrup
- ✓ 2 eggs
- ✓ 200 g (7 oz) Pecan nuts
- ✓ 15 g (3 tsp) Butter
- ✓ 1 Teaspoon
- ✓ Unsweetened cocoa powder

Directions:

Let's start with the base: pour the flour and the cold butter cut into pieces into the cup of a food processor, then blend quickly until you get a sandy mixture.

Pour the mixture into a bowl and add the cold water, a teaspoon of apple cider vinegar and a pinch of salt. Knead quickly with your hands until a homogeneous but not too smooth mixture is obtained. Cover with cling film and leave to rest in the refrigerator for at least an hour.

In the meantime, blend half of the Pecan nuts until they are reduced to flour. Coarsely chop the other half, keeping some aside for decoration.

In a bowl pour the eggs, coconut sugar and brown sugar, and mix using an electric whisk.
Add the maple syrup while continuing to whip with the whisk.

At this point pour the melted (cold) butter with a teaspoon of bitter cocoa powder, a pinch of salt and the pecan nuts reduced to flour. Always work with electric whips.
Finally add the coarsely chopped pecans and mix well.

On a lightly floured surface, roll out the dough, helping yourself with a rolling pin, to a thickness of about 3-4 millimeters.

Place the rolled out base on a previously buttered and floured (or lined with parchment paper) tart pan with a diameter of 20-22 cm (8 inches) and pierce the base of the cake with the prongs of a fork.

Pour the walnut filling inside and finally decorate the surface with other pecans.

Bake in a static oven preheated to 170 °C (340 °F) for about 50 minutes.

Take out the cake and let it cool completely before serving.

CORNELIUS FUDGE CHEESECAKE

Difficulty: Medium

Time: 90 minutes

Serves: 6 people

Ingredients:

For the Base:

- ✓ 10 Dry Biscuits
- ✓ 90 gr (6 tbsp) melted butter
- ✓ 30 gr (2 tbsp) white sugar
- ✓ 1 pinch of fine salt

For the filling:

- ✓ 1 kg (4 cups) Spreadable Cheese
- ✓ 250 gr (1 cup) white sugar

- ✓ 245 gr (1 cup) sour cream
- ✓ 6 large eggs
- ✓ 1 tablespoon of vanilla extract

For the decoration:

- ✓ 120 gr (4 oz) of cream
- ✓ 100 gr (3.5 oz) white sugar
- ✓ 1 tablespoon of butter
- ✓ 1 tablespoon of light corn syrup
- ✓ 1 teaspoon of vanilla extract
- ✓ Pecan Walnuts

Directions:

To prepare the base of the Pecan Nut Cheesecake, take the biscuits and crumble them roughly, then finely chop them with a mixer.

Add the butter, sugar and salt in the mixer, then work until a homogeneous mixture is obtained. Take an open cake tin and grease it, then form the biscuit base by pressing lightly with your hands to obtain a compact and well-leveled surface. Bake in a preheated oven at 160 °C (320 °F) for about 10 minutes to harden, then leave to cool.

For the filling, put the spread cheese, sugar and sour cream in a mixer and mix until a smooth and homogeneous mixture is obtained. Add the eggs, vanilla and some chopped walnuts and mix them with the rest of the mixture.

Take the cake tin and wrap it on the outside with aluminum foil, then pour the mixture you have prepared on the base, leveling the surface well.

Take a baking sheet and place it inside the cake tin, then fill the pan with hot water until it is halfway through the pan.

Bake for about 1 hour and 10 minutes or at least until the edge of the cake has become solid, while the center has remained slightly softer. To check that the cooking is correct, move the cake a little to see if the center moves slightly.

At this point, turn off the oven and slightly open the door for a few seconds to let the heat escape. Then close the oven and leave the cake inside for about an hour to rest.

After this time, remove the cake from the oven and let it cool completely, then put it in the refrigerator overnight to make it firm.

Before removing the cake from the refrigerator, prepare the toppings:

Line a baking sheet with parchment paper and distribute the nuts evenly, then bake in a preheated oven at 180 ° C (360 °F) for about 15 minutes or at least until they have darkened. Remove from the oven and let cool.

In the meantime, take a medium-sized saucepan and heat the cream, butter, corn syrup, vanilla and salt over medium heat, stirring well to prevent sticking to the pan. When the mixture is hot, lower the heat to low.

Take a non-stick pan and cook the sugar until it is completely dissolved, then when it becomes caramel, remove the mixture with the cream from the heat and add the caramel, stirring to mix all the ingredients.

At this point put everything back on the gas over medium heat and cook for about 2 minutes, then let it cool completely.

Coarsely chop the walnuts, then remove the cake from the pan with the help of a knife. Spread the walnuts and caramel on top of the cake and serve.

SLYTHERIN'S PISTACHIO CAKE

Difficulty: Easy

Time: 2 hours

Serves: 6 people

Ingredients:

For the cake:

- ✓ 400 g (1 and ½ cups) sugar
- ✓ 400 g (1 and ½ cups) soft butter
- ✓ 6 eggs
- ✓ 250 g (1 cup) icing sugar
- ✓ 300 g (10,5 oz) flour
- ✓ 100 g (3,5 oz) bitter cocoa
- ✓ 250 g (1 cup) chopped walnuts

For the glaze:

- ✓ 30 g (2 tbsp) bitter cocoa
- ✓ 90 g (6 tbsp) icing sugar
- ✓ 4 or 5 spoons whole milk
- ✓ pistachios to taste

Directions:

Whisk the sugar with the soft butter in a large bowl with an electric whisk until it becomes a frothy and soft compound. Add one egg at a time, working well with the whisk at low speed, then gradually add the icing sugar.

Separately sift the flour and cocoa and add them to the dough bowl with the help of a spatula. Add the chopped walnuts and mix well. Spread the mixture with a spoon in a greased and floured mold.

Preheat the oven to 180 °C (360 °F) and bake for about 50 minutes or until the surface of the cake is solid. Let the cake cool for at least 3 hours before removing it from the mold, it might break otherwise.

To prepare the glaze, mix all the ingredients in a bowl with the help of a hand whisk. Place the cake on a wire rack and pour the glaze over it. When the glaze is still soft, add the crumbles pistachios.

HERMIONE'S FUDGY BROWNIES

Difficulty: Medium

Time: 90 minutes

Serves: 6 people

Ingredients:

For the cake:

- ✓ 200 g (7 oz) dark chocolate
- ✓ 160 g (5,5 oz) granulated sugar
- ✓ 120 g (4 oz) butter
- ✓ 75 g (5 tbsp) flour
- ✓ 60 g (4 tbsp) chopped hazelnuts
- ✓ 3 whole eggs
- ✓ a pinch of salt
- ✓ 1 vanilla bean

For the salted caramel:

- ✓ 160 gr (5.5 oz) granulated sugar
- ✓ 100 ml (3.5 fl oz) fresh cream
- ✓ 1 knob of butter
- ✓ a drop of water
- ✓ half a teaspoon of salt
- ✓ 1 teaspoon honey

Directions:

Let's start by preparing the salted caramel: pour the caster sugar, a few drops of water and the honey in a saucepan. Cook on low heat without stirring too much.

In the meantime, heat the cream to a boil and when the sugar is well caramelized (the color must be amber), remove it from the heat and add half the hot cream, butter and salt.
Stir quickly with a hand whisk and stir in the remaining hot cream.
Cook for a couple more minutes, until it has thickened and then let it cool in a glass jar.

Melt the butter and dark chocolate in a water bath (main-marie)
Once dissolved and well blended, let cool.
Whip the eggs (egg yolks + egg whites) with sugar using an electric whisk until they have swollen and doubled in volume. Add a pinch of salt.
Cut the vanilla bean, remove the seeds and add them to the mix.
Pour the melted butter and chocolate into the mixture. Mix well and finally add the flour.
Stir in half the chopped hazelnuts and then pour the dough into a greased and floured pan.
Sprinkle the remaining hazelnuts on the surface and cook in the oven, at 180° C (360° F) for 35 minutes.
Let cool completely and sprinkle with salted caramel

Hermione's Tips:

For a super delicious effect, serve with a scoop of va nilla ice cream and a chocolate topping.

BUTTERBEER CAKE

Difficulty: Hard

Time: 150 minutes

Serves: 6 people

Ingredients:

For the base:

- ✓ 4 eggs at room temperature
- ✓ 120 g (4 oz) sugar
- ✓ a teaspoon vanilla extract
- ✓ 120 g (4 oz) flour
- ✓ a pinch of salt
- ✓ 20 g (4 tsp) melted butter (cooled down)

For the salted caramel cream:

- ✓ 250 g (1 cup) sugar
- ✓ 120 g (4 oz) butter
- ✓ 200 g (7 oz) fresh cream
- ✓ 10 g (2 tsp) salt
- ✓ 10 macarons
- ✓ Popcorn

For the meringue butter cream:

- ✓ 150 g (5 oz) egg whites
- ✓ 200 g (7 oz) icing sugar
- ✓ 250 g (1 cup) butter at room temperature

Directions:

Sift the flour with the salt and melt the butter in the microwave.

Whip the eggs with the sugar and vanilla using an electric whisk until the mixture triples in volume.

Add the flour and incorporate it into the mixture, stirring gently, with a spatula, from the bottom up. Pour the cooled melted butter along the side of the bowl and mix thoroughly again, trying not to disassemble the compound. This is a very important step if you want to keep a frothy mixture that will allow you to have a swollen and soft dough.

Preheat the oven to 180° C (360° F) and pour the dough into the mold and bake for about 30/40 minutes. Check the cooking with a toothpick.

Remove from the oven, turn the sponge cake upside down on a sheet of parchment paper, dusted with granulated sugar to prevent it from sticking, and let it cool completely.

For the caramel cream start by melting the sugar in a saucepan. Set the heat to medium and let the sugar melt on its own: DO NOT STIR but simply rotate the pan every now and then to move the sugar.

When the sugar has completely melted and taken on a golden color, mix with a whisk and turn off the heat immediately. Add the chopped cold butter and salt, mixing well without interruption. This will stop the caramel from cooking any further.

Bring the cream to the boil and when the butter has completely melted pour it on the caramel, stirring quickly to obtain a smooth and velvety sauce, let it rest in the fridge.

For the meringue butter cream, pour the egg whites and sugar into a bowl and heat the mixture in a water bath (bain-marie) until it reaches a temperature of 55° C (130° F).

Once the temperature is reached, remove the bowl from the water bath and whisk at maximum speed until a frothy mixture is obtained.

Add the butter in small pieces one at a time, whipping at medium speed, until a smooth and homogeneous cream is obtained. Refrigerate until ready for use.

Let's compose the cake: cut the sponge cake into three or four layers (depending on the height of the pan you used) and place the first layer on the bottom.

Insert both the butter and caramel cream into two pastry bags.

Create a first layer of butter cream trying to make a small cornice: in the center of this cornice create a second layer of caramel cream, crumble over some macarons and cover with another layer of butter cream.

Smooth the surface well with the help of a spatula trying to level the edges in order to obtain a single layer of butter cream.

Repeat the same operation for the following layers. Place the last layer and cover the whole cake with the meringue butter cream with the help of a spatula.

Let it rest in the refrigerator for a few hours.

Take a part of the caramel cream, heat it in the microwave to make it liquid again and with the help of a teaspoon let it run along the edges.

Whip the rest of the caramel cream and with the help of a pastry bag decorate the cake at your leisure with tufts of cream, some macarons and some caramel covered popcorn.

Hermione's Tips:

If you like a more humid consistency I recommend you to slightly wet the layers with a vanilla bath.

If at the time of filling the caramel cream turns out to be too thick, heat it slightly in the microwave: it must have the consistency of a cream.

To obtain a very white butter cream, add a few drops of white dye.

HARRY'S BREAKFAST

Difficulty: Easy

Time: 40 minutes

Serves: 4 people

Ingredients:

For the pancakes:

- ✓ 120 g (4 oz) flour
- ✓ 2 medium eggs
- ✓ 200 g (7 oz) whole milk
- ✓ 20 g (4 tsp) butter
- ✓ 5 g (1 tsp) baking powder
- ✓ 15 g (3 tsp) sugar

For the caramel sauce and seasoning:

- ✓ 250 g (1 cup) sugar
- ✓ 120 g (4 oz) butter
- ✓ 200 g (7 oz) fresh liquid cream
- ✓ 10 g (2 tsp) fine salt
- ✓ 300 g (10.5 oz) fresh cream
- ✓ 3 bananas
- ✓ 10 walnuts

Directions:

Begin by gently melting the butter in a saucepan and letting it cool.

Separate the egg whites from the yolks, placing them in a bowl. Beat the egg yolks with a whisk and, continuing to mix, add the melted butter and the milk. Sift the flour with the baking powder and add it one spoon at a time, always mixing with a whisk.

Whisk the egg whites with the sugar and when they are white and frothy, add them a little at a time to the egg and flour mixture, with gentle movements from top to bottom, to avoid dismantling the mass.

Heat a non-stick pan and grease it with a knob of butter. Pour the batter with a ladle. Without touching the dough, which will spread on its own, let the pancake cook until the base is golden brown and bubbles will appear on the surface. Turn it with the help of a spatula and also brown the other side. Proceed in this way until all the batter is finished and gradually arrange the pancakes on a serving plate.

To make the salted caramel sauce, put the sugar in a saucepan with a fairly wide and thick base. Let the sugar melt on its own without ever stirring, simply swirling the pan every so often. When the sugar is completely melted and has taken on a golden color, mix it with a steel whisk and turn off the heat immediately, to avoid burning it. Immediately add the butter into small pieces and the salt, while continuing to whisk, and when the butter has melted, add the cream and whisk until a smooth and velvety sauce is obtained. Transfer the caramel sauce to a bowl and let it cool before using it.

Finally, whip the whipped cream and cut the bananas into thin slices for the filling.

Serve the pancakes with salted caramel, bananas and walnuts forming a "turret" and decorate with the cream, the chopped walnuts and a generous spoonful of salted caramel sauce.

Hermione's Tips:

It is possible to enrich pancakes in many different ways: by adding ricotta to the dough, but also by preparing them with chocolate cream. Another delicious idea is to make colored pancakes: the addition of matcha green tea, for example, allows you to make green pancakes, while the addition of turmeric intensifies their yellow color.

With the use of gluten-free flours such as buckwheat, corn and rice it is also possible to make gluten-free pancakes

DUMBLEDORE'S PUMPKIN CHEESECAKE

Difficulty: Medium

Time: 90 minutes

Serves: 6 people

Ingredients:

For the base:

300 g (10.5 oz) dry biscuits

150 g (5 oz) butter

2 tablespoons of brown sugar

For the cream:

- ✓ 3 eggs
- ✓ 150 g (5 oz) sugar

- ✓ 300 g (10.5 oz) fresh cheese
- ✓ 250 g (1 cup) mascarpone
- ✓ 400 g (1 and ½ cup) pumpkin flesh
- ✓ 45 ml (3 tbsp) milk
- ✓ 75 g (5 tbsp) flour

For the glaze & decorations:

- ✓ 45 g (3 tbsp) dark chocolate
- ✓ 200 ml (7 fl oz) of sour cream
- ✓ 2 large spoons of granulated sugar
- ✓ 1 tablespoon of vanilla essence
- ✓ Berries
- ✓ Walnuts

Directions:

Put the biscuits in a bag and crush them into powder with the help of a rolling pin. You can also use a mixer, to speed up the operation.

In a bowl mix the biscuits, melted butter and brown sugar.

Put the obtained mixture in a hinged mold with a diameter of 22-24 cm (8 inches) lined with parchment paper and put the mold in the fridge for at least one hour.

In a saucepan, cook the pumpkin (cut into small pieces) with half a glass of water until the desired tenderness is reached. Add the milk and blend it with an immersion blender.

In a bowl, whisk the eggs and sugar for 5 minutes, until a frothy mixture is obtained. Add mascarpone and fresh cheese, then the pureed pumpkin. Finally add the sieved flour.

Take the mold from the fridge and pour the mixture into it. Bake in a preheated oven at 160° C (320° F) for about 45-60 minutes.

Soften the sour cream in a bowl, add the sugar and stir until a soft cream is obtained.
Take the cheesecake, spread all of the cream on the surface and bake at 160° C (320° F) for 10 more minutes.

Take the pan out of the oven, let it cool completely (about two hours) and refrigerate for at least 6 hours. Add the dried fruit and berries topping and serve

QUIDDITCH TRADITIONAL CAKE

Difficulty: Medium

Time: 1 hour

Serves: 6 people

Ingredients:

- 250 gr (1 cup) pumpkin
- 2 eggs
- 200 gr (7 oz) flour
- 1 sachet yeast
- 45 ml (3 tbsp) milk
- 75 gr (5 tbsp) butter
- 120 gr (4 oz) sugar
- 1 pinch of salt

- ✓ 300 ml (10.5 fl oz) custard
- ✓ 120 ml (4 fl oz) fresh cream
- ✓ 2 tablespoons of icing sugar
- ✓ Candy corn

Directions:

Begin by baking the pumpkin in the oven at 180 ° C (360 °F) for 20 minutes, then blend with the blender to obtain a smooth purée.

Beat the eggs with the sugar until the mixture is swollen and frothy, add the warm milk and the melted butter and then add the salt. Add the pumpkin puree and then add sieved yeast and flour. Mix everything so that you have a creamy and lump-free mixture.

Grease and flour a cake mold, pour the mixture and bake the cake in a hot oven at 180° C (360° F) for 35 minutes.

Whip the cream with the sugar using an electric whisk and then add it to the cold custard with a spatula, a little at a time.

Cut the cake into three layers, put the cream between the layers and garnish with the remaining cream and some candy corns, chocolate or sugar.

DURMSTRANG FAMOUS CAKE

Difficulty: Hard

Time: 150 minutes

Serves: 6 people

Ingredients:

- 500 g (2 cups) flour
- 90 g (6 tbsp) butter
- 170 g (6 oz) chestnut honey or forest honeydew
- 2 eggs
- 1 spoonful of vodka
- 2 teaspoons of baking soda
- 200 ml (7 fl oz) whole milk
- 160 g (5.5 oz) acacia honey

- ✓ a pinch of vanillin powder (vanilla extract)
- ✓ 500 g (1 cup) of mascarpone

Directions:

To prepare the Durmstrang cake, you must first of all take care of the biscuit bases: melt 60 g of butter in a water bath (bain-marie) then add 170 g of dark honey, 2 eggs and a spoonful of vodka, then mix with a hand whisk until you will have obtained a smooth and lump free compound.

Cook the obtained compound but be careful not to overheat too much, because the eggs do not have to cook. Remove it from the heat as soon as it is hot and the ingredients have mixed well.

Pour the mixture into a large bowl and add 2 teaspoons of baking soda, then whip it with an electric whisk until it has doubled in volume.

At this point, incorporate 250 g of flour, mixing it a little at a time and mixing everything with a hand whisk or spatula. As soon as you have obtained a dough that is too thick to mix, add the remaining flour and work it with your hands until you get a smooth dough that does not stick to your hands.

Wrap the dough ball in plastic wrap and let it cool completely, keeping it at room temperature.

While the dough cools, prepare the honey condensed milk: in a saucepan on low heat, put 200 ml of whole milk, 160 g of acacia honey, 30 g of butter and a pinch of vanillin powder, and as soon as the mixture starts to boil, let it cook for about 15-20 minutes, stirring constantly with a spatula or a hand whisk.

Once ready, turn off the heat and let the honey condensed milk cool completely.

Divide the dough into 9 equal parts, then spread each piece of dough on a floured work surface, until it forms very thin (about 3 mm) circular sheets, wide enough to be able to cut disks of 20 centimeters (8 inches) in diameter.

To cut the discs, you can help yourself with the bottom of a 20 cm (8 inches) hinged mold, resting it on the sheet and cutting with a knife or pizza wheel.

Keep the scraps aside and cook the discs, one or two at a time, in a preheated oven at 180° C (360° F) for about 6-7 minutes or until they are golden brown (cooking times may change from oven to oven. When ready, take them out of the oven and let them cool completely.

Also bake the dough scraps, without worrying too much about the shape, because they will then be crumbled. Once cooked, let them cool, then crumble them coarsely, putting them in a plastic bag and crushing them with a rolling pin.

As soon as the condensed milk is cold, prepare the cream to stuff the cake: in a bowl beat 500 g of mascarpone together with all the honey condensed milk, until you get a rather fluid and creamy mixture, then keep it aside.

Now you just have to assemble the cake: place a sheet of baking paper on a serving plate, then place a biscuit disc on top and spread it evenly with 2-3 abundant spoons of cream, then place the second biscuit on top, pressing it lightly and spread this too with another 2-3 abundant spoons of cream. Don't worry if the cream comes out from the sides, it's normal and that's the way it should be.

Proceed in this way with all 9 layers, then spread the remaining cream also on the last layer, leveling the cream that has come out along the perimeter of the cake with a spatula.

Cover your cake with the crumbled biscuits, both on the top and on the sides, then hold the biscuit tower firmly with the help of two or three wooden sticks by sticking them directly in the cake.

Transfer the cake to the refrigerator and let it rest overnight (better yet 24 hours). Once ready, carefully remove the sticks and serve

RON'S FAVOURITE PLUMCAKE

Difficulty: Easy

Time: 1 hour

Serves: 4 people

Ingredients:

For the cake:

- ✓ 200 g (7 oz) flour
- ✓ 75 g (5 tbsp) sugar
- ✓ 100 g (3,5 oz) almonds
- ✓ 3 eggs
- ✓ 150 ml (5 fl oz) sunflower oil
- ✓ 1 pinch of salt
- ✓ 1/2 sachet of yeast

- ✓ 1 kg (4 cups) apples
- ✓ 1 teaspoon cinnamon

For the frosting:

- ✓ 150 g (5 oz) cream cheese
- ✓ 20 g (4 tsp) butter
- ✓ 10 g (2 tsp) honey
- ✓ 4 drops of vanilla extract
- ✓ milk to soften if necessary

Directions:

Beat the eggs with the sugar, until a foamy mixture is obtained

Add the oil and then all the powdered ingredients (sifted flour, baking powder, pinch of salt, and cinnamon). Mix everything together and add the chopped almonds and the diced apples (keep half of the apples aside to decorate the cake on the surface).

Line a plumcake-shaped mold with parchment paper and pour the dough. Place the apple slices on top of the dough and bake at 180° C (360° F) for 30/40 minutes.

For the frosting, put all the ingredients (honey, vanilla, cream cheese and butter) in a mixer and blend at medium speed for 2-3 minutes: you need to obtain a thick cream. If it is too dry, add a few drops of milk.

Spread the frosting on the cake, let rest for 10 minutes and serve.

CAULDRON CAKE

Difficulty: Medium

Time: 90 minutes

Serves: 6 people

Ingredients:

- ✓ 4 eggs
- ✓ 250 g (1 cup) flour
- ✓ 150 g (5 oz) sugar
- ✓ 150 ml (5 fl oz) milk
- ✓ 100 g (3.5 oz) sweetened cocoa
- ✓ 100 ml (3.5 fl oz) vegetable oil
- ✓ 1 teaspoon vanilla extract
- ✓ 8 g (1 tsp) baking powder

- ✓ 1 pinch of salt
- ✓ 150 ml (5 fl oz) fresh cream
- ✓ 100 g (3.5 oz) dark chocolate
- ✓ 30 g (2 tbsp) butter

Directions:

In a bowl, whisk the eggs and sugar until they become light and frothy.

Add the sifted cocoa, then the oil and milk and finally the flour, little by little, stirring until a smooth and lump-free batter is obtained.
Finally, add the vanilla extract, salt and baking powder and mix well.

Grease the mold carefully or line it with parchment paper.

Bake at 180° C (360° F) in a preheated oven for about 45 minutes. Use a toothpick to check if ready.

Remove from the oven and let cool for 10 minutes, then take the cake out of the mold and let it cool completely on a wire rack.

To prepare the chocolate ganache, cut the chocolate with a knife and put it in a bowl.
Heat the cream together with the butter, without bringing to a boil.
When it is very hot, pour it on the chocolate, cover the container with a plate or a lid and leave it to rest for about 5 minutes. This will melt the chocolate.
Remove the lid and mix everything until a smooth and shiny cream is obtained.

Strain the ganache on the cakes and garnish with fresh fruit, sugar or other chocolate decorations.

DURLEYS'S DOUGHNUTS

Difficulty: Medium

Time: 1 hour

Serves: 6 people

Ingredients:

For the doughnuts:

- ✓ 500 g (1 cup) flour
- ✓ 2 yolks
- ✓ 300 g (10.5 oz) sugar
- ✓ 150 ml (5 fl oz) milk
- ✓ 75 g (5 tbsp) butter
- ✓ 30 g (2 tbsp) brewer's yeast
- ✓ salt to taste

For the stuffing & decoration:

- ✓ jam to taste
- ✓ icing sugar

Directions:

Let's start with the dough: pour the milk in a bowl and add the yeast. Also add about 120 g of flour, mix and set aside in a warm environment for half an hour.

Once this is done, transfer the mixture to the planetary mixer and add the yolks (at room temperature) one at a time, the remaining flour, butter (soft) and sugar.

All the ingredients will be added little by little only when the quantity added before has been perfectly incorporated. Also add a pinch of salt and work until it forms an elastic and very soft compound. Transfer the dough, which will still be sticky, on a sheet of transparent film and let it rise for at least 2 hours, so that it doubles its initial volume.

Only at this point can you transfer the mixture to the floured work surface and roll out until it is about 1 cm thick. Make some discs using a mould.

Fill the discs with a teaspoon of jam, wet the edges with water and seal by covering with another disc of pasta. Press well on the edges and then put on a floured tray. Cover with a cloth and let rise for another hour

Now we're ready to cook the doughnuts: bring the peanut oil to a temperature of 165° C (330° F). Cook for a few minutes on each until golden. Once cooked, quickly pass them on a sheet of kitchen paper to eliminate the excess oil.

Sprinkle with sugar and rest for 10-15 minutes before serving.

SLUG CLUB DESSERT

Difficulty: Easy

Time: 30 Minutes

Serves: 4 people

Ingredients:

- 500 g (2 cups) ladyfinger biscuits
- 4 eggs
- 200 g (7 oz) sugar
- 45 g (3 tbsp) flour
- 500 ml (2 cups) milk
- vanilla bean
- cocoa powder
- 250 ml (1 cup) liqueur

- ✓ strawberries and blueberries

Directions:

In a large bowl, mix the yolks with the sugar until the sugar has dissolved and the mixture has turned pale yellow. Add the flour and mix until everything is well blended.

In a saucepan over low heat, heat the milk and the vanilla bean. After boiling, remove the vanilla bean and gently pour the milk into the egg mixture, stirring constantly until a soft and uniform consistency is obtained.

Pour the mixture back into the saucepan over low heat. Keep stirring until the custard cooks and thickens.

Set aside a third of the cream and add cocoa powder.

Pour some Alchermes liqueur (or another liqueur, like brandy) into a bowl and dip the ladyfingers. In a large pan with high sides, pour some custard, then add a layer of biscuits soaked in liqueur and fruit such as blueberries and strawberries. Add a layer of chocolate custard, then another layer of soaked biscuits and continue to the desired height.

Refrigerate for at least 2 hours before serving. Garnish with fruit on top.

HOGWARTS PUDDING

Difficulty: Medium

Time: 1 hour

Serves: 6 people

Ingredients:

For the pudding:

- ✓ Whole milk 500 g (2 cups)
- ✓ Sugar 75 g (5 tbsp)
- ✓ Corn starch 60 g (4 tbsp)
- ✓ Eggs 3
- ✓ Vanilla 1 berry
- ✓ Raspberries to decorate

For the cream:

- ✓ 500 ml (2 cups) Partially skimmed milk
- ✓ 120 g (4 oz) sugar
- ✓ 3 egg yolks
- ✓ 100 g (3,5 oz) Dark chocolate
- ✓ 45 g (3 tbsp) flour (or corn starch if you want to make the cream gluten free)

Directions:

In a large saucepan, pour the milk, add the vanilla bean and heat without bringing to a boil.
In a large bowl add the eggs and sugar and work until a frothy mixture is obtained. Add the corn starch and mix well.

Add the milk, taking care not to create lumps. Once mixed, transfer the mixture to a pot and bring to the heat. Stir continuously for 10 minutes or until the pudding has thickened. Transfer the mixture to the molds and leave to cool in the fridge for 3 hours.

To make the cream, put the yolks and sugar in a bowl and work with an electric whisk for a few minutes until you have a clear and frothy mixture.

Add the flour, one spoon at a time and then the milk until it is smooth and lump-free.

Transfer everything to a pan and thicken over low heat. From the moment it starts boiling, cook for about 3-4 minutes, stirring constantly to prevent sticking.

Once ready, turn off the heat, add the chopped dark chocolate and stir until the chocolate has completely melted. Transfer the cream to a bowl, cover with cling film and let it cool.

Turn out the puddings and serve by decorating with a chocolate glaze and some raspberries

POMONA SPROUT SECRET RECIPE

Difficulty: Medium

Time: 90 minutes

Serves: 6 people

Ingredients:

- ✓ 250 g (1 cup) dry biscuits
- ✓ 120 g (4 oz) melted butter
- ✓ 100 g (3,5 oz) chopped butter
- ✓ 100 g (3,5 oz) brown sugar
- ✓ 500 g (2 cups) condensed milk
- ✓ 4 medium-small bananas
- ✓ 500 ml (2 cups) cold, fresh liquid cream from the refrigerator
- ✓ 5 g (1 tsp) Jelly

- ✓ 45 g (3 tbsp) icing sugar
- ✓ 100 g (3,5 oz) dark chocolate
- ✓ 45 g (3 tbsp) white chocolate

Directions:

To prepare the Banoffee pie, start by preparing the biscuit base: in a mixer finely chop 250 g of biscuits, then put them in a large bowl and add 120 g of melted butter. Mix well.

Transfer this crumbly mixture into a tart mold (removable bottom) with a diameter of about 24 centimeters (9.5 inches) and crush it well both on the bottom and on the sides of the mold.
If you prefer, you can use a hinged mold, but in that case you will first have to line it with parchment paper.

Put the mold in the freezer for 15-20 minutes and in the meantime make the caramel toffee cream: in a saucepan, melt 100g of butter over low heat for a couple of minutes, together with 100 g of brown sugar.
Add 500 g of condensed milk and cook for 15-20 minutes, or at least until you have obtained a thick and full-bodied cream, brown in color. Turn off the heat and transfer the cream to a bowl, leaving it to cool.

Soften 5 g of jelly in a bowl filled with cold water for 10 minutes and as soon as it is soft, drain it, squeeze it very well and put it in a saucepan over low heat together with two or three tablespoons of fresh liquid cream. As soon as the jelly dissolves, turn off the heat and let the mixture cool.

In a large bowl whisk all the remaining fresh liquid cream (therefore just under 500 ml) together with 50 g of icing sugar and the warmed cream and gelatine mixture, until you have obtained a swollen and well mounted mass.

Once ready, transfer the whipped cream to the refrigerator and proceed with the assembly of your Banoffee pie.

Take the biscuit and butter base out of the freezer and pour the caramel toffee cream inside, then using a spatula, level it well on the surface.

Peel the 4 bananas and slice them into thin slices, then arrange them on the caramel, concentrically and without overlapping them too much.

Fill a pastry bag with whipped cream and cover the bananas with tufts. If you prefer you can garnish banana slices and chocolate flakes.

At this point your banoffee pie is ready to be eaten immediately, but if you don't have to serve it immediately, you can keep it in the refrigerator for up to two days.

GRYFFINDOR HOUSE CAKE

Difficulty: Medium

Time: 90 minutes

Serves: 4 people

Ingredients:

- 185 gr (6,5 oz) butter
- 175 g (6 oz) sugar
- 3 eggs
- 175 gr (6 oz) flour
- 6 g (1 tsp) yeast
- 45 ml (3 tbsp) milk
- red dye
- apricot jam to taste
- marzipan or sugar paste to taste

Directions:

Put the softened butter in a bowl, add sugar and whip it using an electric whisk.

Then add the eggs, which you will have previously beaten in another bowl.

At this point, add the sifted flour and baking powder, mixing with the whisk. Add milk gradually to soften the dough. The consistency will seem a little too fluid, but trust me, it is only because the mixture has incorporated a lot of air. If you like, add a few drops of almond aroma, which will go well with the marzipan.

Divide the mixture in two, and in one half add a little red dye (very little, to get a pinkish hue.

Now you need to bake the cake: take a rectangular baking dish (about 25x35cm or 10x14 inches) and cover it with parchment paper. Cut two more pieces and create two different "linings" along the length of the baking dish: pour the two doughs separately

Bake at 180°C (360° F) and cook for 35/40 minutes; remove from the oven and let cool.

Take the two halves of cake, which should have rectangular shape, and remove the crust using a sharp knife. Then cut them so as to obtain two parallelepipeds per color: assemble them like in the picture, spreading them with apricot jam to allow the 4 pieces to adhere well.

Roll out the marzipan or sugar paste, smear the cake with jam and cover everything.

Printed in Great Britain
by Amazon